Y0-IWC-607

OUR EXTREME EARTH

FOSSILS

REBECCA FELIX

Consulting Editor, Diane Craig, M.A./Reading Specialist

Sandcastle

An Imprint of Abdo Publishing
abdopublishing.com

abdopublishing.com

Published by Abdo Publishing, a division of ABDO, PO Box 398166, Minneapolis, Minnesota 55439. Copyright © 2018 by Abdo Consulting Group, Inc. International copyrights reserved in all countries. No part of this book may be reproduced in any form without written permission from the publisher. SandCastle™ is a trademark and logo of Abdo Publishing.

Printed in the United States of America, North Mankato, Minnesota

102017
012018

THIS BOOK CONTAINS
RECYCLED MATERIALS

Design: Kelly Doudna, Mighty Media, Inc.
Production: Mighty Media, Inc.
Editor: Liz Salzmann
Cover Photographs: iStockphoto, Shutterstock
Interior Photographs: iStockphoto, Shutterstock, Wikimedia Commons

Publisher's Cataloging-in-Publication Data

Names: Felix, Rebecca, author.
Title: Fossils / by Rebecca Felix.
Description: Minneapolis, Minnesota : Abdo Publishing, 2018. | Series: Our extreme earth |
Identifiers: LCCN 2017946506 | ISBN 9781532112232 (lib.bdg.) |
ISBN 9781614799658 (ebook)
Subjects: LCSH: Paleontology--Juvenile literature. | Fossils--Juvenile literature. |
Earth sciences--Juvenile literature.
Classification: DDC 560--dc23
LC record available at https://lccn.loc.gov/2017946506

SandCastle™ Level: Fluent

SandCastle™ books are created by a team of professional educators, reading specialists, and content developers around five essential components—phonemic awareness, phonics, vocabulary, text comprehension, and fluency—to assist young readers as they develop reading skills and strategies and increase their general knowledge. All books are written, reviewed, and leveled for guided reading, early reading intervention, and Accelerated Reader® programs for use in shared, guided, and independent reading and writing activities to support a balanced approach to literacy instruction. The SandCastle™ series has four levels that correspond to early literacy development. The levels are provided to help teachers and parents select appropriate books for young readers.

EMERGING · BEGINNING · TRANSITIONAL · FLUENT

CONTENTS

ABOUT FOSSILS

Earth is full of living things. What happens when they die?

They turn into fossils!

Fossils form slowly. It takes millions of years.

First, an animal dies. Soon, dirt covers it.

Many years go by. More dirt covers the dead animal.

Its soft parts **decay**. Its bones remain.

The **layers** of dirt build up. They create **pressure**.

It turns to rock. The dirt hardens.

Under the layers of rock, the bones turn into fossils.

Plants can also become fossils. These fossils are called imprints.

Millions of years pass. Weather wears away **layers** of dirt.

This brings the fossils near the surface. People can find them.

Mary Anning was a **paleontologist**. She studied fossils. She learned a lot about ancient life on Earth.

People learn a lot from fossils.

They learn about history. They learn about Earth.

THINK ABOUT IT

Fossils teach us about Earth's history. Have you ever seen a fossil?

GLOSSARY

decay – to rot away or break down through a natural process.

layer – one thickness of a material or a substance lying over or under another.

paleontologist – a person who studies fossils and ancient animals and plants.

pressure – the force of something pressing against something else.